Recove
Guilt

MW00834064

Juanita & Dale Ryan

6 Studies for
Groups or Individuals

With Notes for Leaders

☑ LIFE RECOVERY GUIDES

INTERVARSITY PRESS
DOWNERS GROVE, ILLINOIS 60515

InterVarsity Press® is the book-publishing division of InterVarsity Christian Fellowship®, a student movement active on campus at hundreds of universities, colleges and schools of nursing in the United States of America, and a member movement of the International Fellowship of Evangelical Students. For information about local and regional activities, write Public Relations Dept., InterVarsity Christian Fellowship, 6400 Schroeder Rd., P.O. Box 7895, Madison, WI 53707-7895.

All Scripture quotations, unless otherwise indicated, are taken from the HOLY BIBLE, NEW INTERNATIONAL VERSION®. NIV®. Copyright ©1973, 1978, 1984 by International Bible Society. Used by permission of Zondervan Publishing House. All rights reserved.

The Twelve Steps are reprinted with permission of Alcoholics Anonymous World Services, Inc. Permission to reprint and adapt the Twelve Steps does not mean that A.A. has reviewed or approved the contents of this publication, nor that A.A. agrees with the views expressed herein. A.A. is a program of recovery from alcoholism. Use of the Twelve Steps in connection with programs which are patterned after A.A. but which address other problems does not imply otherwise.

Cover illustration: Tim Nyberg

ISBN 0-8308-1163-X

Printed in the United States of America ∞

14	13	12	11	10	9	8	7	6	5	4	3	2	1
04	03	02	01	00	99	98	97	96	95	94	93		

An Invitation to Recovery

Life Recovery Guides are rooted in four basic convictions.

First, we are in need of recovery. The word *recovery* implies that something has gone wrong. Things are not as they should be. We have sinned. We have been sinned against. We are entangled, stuck, bogged down, bound and broken. We need to be healed.

Second, recovery is a commitment to change. Because of this, recovery is a demanding process and often a lengthy one. There are no quick fixes in recovery. It means facing the truth about ourselves, even when that truth is painful. It means giving up our old destructive patterns and learning new life-giving patterns. Recovery means taking responsibility for our lives. It is not easy. It is sometimes painful. And it will take time.

Third, recovery is possible. No matter how hopeless it may seem, no matter how deeply we have been wounded by life or how often we have failed, recovery is possible. Our primary basis for hope in the process of recovery is that God is able to do things which we cannot do ourselves. Recovery is possible because God has committed himself to us.

Finally, these studies are rooted in the conviction that the Bible can be a significant resource for recovery. Many people who have lived through difficult life experiences have had bits of the Bible thrown at their pain as a quick fix or a simplistic solution. As a result, many people expect the Bible to be a barrier to recovery rather than a resource. These studies are based on the belief that the

Bible is not a book of quick fixes and simplistic solutions. It is, on the contrary, a practical and helpful resource for recovery.

We were deeply moved personally by these biblical texts as we worked on this series. We are convinced that the God of the Bible can bring serenity to people whose lives have become unmanageable. If you are looking for resources to help you in your recovery, we invite you to study the Bible with an open mind and heart.

Getting the Most from Life Recovery Guides

Life Recovery Guides are designed to assist you to find out for yourself what the Bible has to say about different aspects of recovery. The texts you will study will be thought-provoking, challenging, inspiring and very personal. It will become obvious that these studies are not designed merely to convince you of the truthfulness of some idea. Rather, they are designed to allow biblical truths to renew your heart and mind.

We want to encourage realistic expectations of these discussion guides. First, they are not intended to be everything-the-Bible-says about any subject. They are not intended to be a systematic presentation of biblical theology.

Second, we want to emphasize that these guides are not intended to provide a recovery program or to be a substitute for professional counseling. If you are in a counseling relationship or are involved in a support group, we pray that these studies will enrich that resource. If you are not in a counseling relationship and your recovery involves long-term issues, we encourage you to consider seeking the assistance of a mental health professional.

What these guides are designed to do is to help you study a series of biblical texts which relate to the process of recovery. Our hope is that they will allow you to discover the Good News for people who are struggling to recover.

There are six studies in each Life Recovery Guide. This should provide you with maximum flexibility in how you use these guides.

Combining the guides in various ways will allow you to adapt them to your time schedule and to focus on the concerns most important to you or your group.

All of the studies in this series use a workbook format. Space is provided for writing answers to each question. This is ideal for personal study and allows group members to prepare in advance for the discussion. The guides also contain leader's notes with suggestions on how to lead a group discussion. The notes provide additional background information on certain questions, give helpful tips on group dynamics and suggest ways to deal with problems that may arise during the discussion. These features enable someone with little or no experience to lead an effective discussion.

Suggestions for Individual Study

1. As you begin each study, pray that God would bring healing and recovery to you through his Word.

2. After spending time in personal reflection, read and reread the passage to be studied.

3. Write your answers in the spaces provided or in a personal journal. Writing can bring clarity and deeper understanding of yourself and of the Bible. For the same reason, we suggest that you write out your prayers at the end of each study.

4. Use the leader's notes at the back of the guide to gain additional insight and information.

5. Share what you are learning with someone you trust. Recovery is empowered by experiences of community.

Suggestions for Group Study

Even if you have already done these studies individually, we strongly encourage you to find some way to do them with a group of other people as well. Although each person's recovery is different, everyone's recovery is empowered by the mutual support and encouragement that can only be found in a one-on-one or a group setting.

Several reminders may be helpful for participants in a group study:

1. Realize that trust grows over time. If opening up in a group setting is risky, realize that you do not have to share more than what feels safe to you. However, taking risks is a necessary part of recovery. So, do participate in the discussion as much as you are able.

2. Be sensitive to the other members of the group. Listen attentively when they talk. You will learn from their insights. If you can, link what you say to the comments of others so the group stays on the topic. Also, be affirming whenever you can. This will encourage some of the more hesitant members of the group to participate.

3. Be careful not to dominate the discussion. We are sometimes so eager to share what we have learned that we do not leave opportunity for others to respond. By all means participate! But allow others to do so as well.

4. Expect God to teach you through the passage being discussed and through the other members of the group. Pray that you will have a profitable time together.

5. We recommend that groups follow a few basic guidelines, and that these guidelines be read at the beginning of each discussion session. The guidelines, which you may wish to adapt to your situation, are:

    a. Anything said in the group is considered confidential and will not be discussed outside the group unless specific permission is given to do so.

    b. We will provide time for each person present to talk if he or she feels comfortable doing so.

    c. We will talk about ourselves and our own situations, avoiding conversation about other people.

    d. We will listen attentively to each other.

    e. We will be very cautious about giving advice.

    f. We will pray for each other.

If you are the discussion leader, you will find additional suggestions and helpful ideas for each study in the leader's notes. These are found at the back of the guide.

Recovering from Guilt

Guilt is a painful internal alarm that alerts us to the fact that we have sinned. It is a private anguish which prods us to acknowledge our destructive behaviors toward ourselves and toward others.

We don't like emotional pain of any kind. Grief, anger and fear are difficult enough. But, for many of us, guilt is the most difficult emotional pain of all. Unfortunately, guilt is a necessary kind of pain. Like all painful emotions, guilt is a distress signal that is meant to warn us that something is wrong. We need to pay attention to this warning. If we do not pay attention, we will continue in our destructive ways.

It is important to remember that the word *guilt* is often misused. We say "I feel guilty," for example, about things that have nothing to do with wrongdoing. In fact, sometimes we say "I feel guilty" for behaviors that are good and healthy. For instance, we may say "I feel guilty" when we say no to overcommitments. What we are feeling, however, is not guilt. We are experiencing the anxiety which comes when we are not able to meet our own or other people's expectations. The people we disappoint when we say no may be angry with us.

They may tell us we have failed them. But our behavior is not a violation of our conscience or of God's law. It is, rather, honest, self-respectful behavior. When we say "I feel guilty" for this kind of behavior, we are experiencing what some writers refer to as "false guilt."

The experience of guilt which is the focus for this Life Recovery Guide is the experience of true guilt. We want to focus on recovery from the pain we experience when we have lied, cheated, verbally attacked another person, had an affair, or spent the family's money on our drug of choice. We want to focus on recovery from the guilt that comes when we have done harm to ourselves or to others.

How do we recover from guilt? In order to recover from guilt we need to seek forgiveness. At the heart of the Christian faith is the promise of forgiveness and healing. The reality of our guilt and of God's provision of forgiveness in Jesus is woven throughout the biblical text. The Bible tells us that when we acknowledge our sins and turn from them, God forgives us.

I will forgive their wickedness and will remember their sins no more. (Jeremiah 31:34)

He was pierced for our transgressions,
     he was crushed for our iniquities;
the punishment that brought us peace was upon him,
     and by his wounds we are healed. (Isaiah 53:5)

You see, at just the right time, when we were still powerless, Christ died for the ungodly. . . . God demonstrates his own love for us in this: While we were still sinners, Christ died for us. (Romans 5:6, 8)

If we claim to be without sin, we deceive ourselves and the truth is not in us. If we confess our sins, he is faithful and just and will forgive us our sins and purify us from all unrighteousness. (1 John 1:8-9)

In spite of this promise of God's mercy and forgiveness, however, we almost always experience fear at the same time as we experience guilt. As a consequence, instead of confessing our sin, we hide our guilt from ourselves and from others. Because we expect condemnation instead of grace, we run from our guilt, allowing it to separate us from ourselves, from God and from others.

God calls us instead to face our guilt, to acknowledge our failure and to accept the help and forgiveness offered to us in Christ. It is only then that the estrangement can be repaired; it is only then that we will experience an opportunity to change and grow and heal.

It is our experience that the Twelve Steps of Alcoholics Anonymous provide a rich resource of practical application of the biblical truths about the process of recovery from guilt. The biblical foundations for the first three steps of the Twelve Steps of Alcoholics Anonymous are examined in the Life Recovery Guide *Recovery from Addiction*. These first steps help us to face the reality of our powerlessness and lead us to a face-to-face encounter with God. Working through the first three steps can be a life-changing experience for people who experience guilt. If you have not already done so, we strongly encourage you to experience the healing of the first three steps before beginning this study. The first three steps are, however, only the beginning of the adventure.

Steps four through nine of the Twelve Steps of Alcoholics Anonymous bring us into a new arena of challenge, opportunity, self-discovery and personal change. In the steps covered by this Life Recovery Guide we will make a moral inventory, confess our wrongdoings to God, to ourselves and to another human being, examine our character flaws and ask God to remove them, and make a list of people we have harmed and seek to make amends. These studies are designed to help you as you work through steps four through nine of a Twelve-Step program. We strongly encourage you to participate in a support group as part of your recovery journey. The wisdom, strength and hope of others can help you through the most difficult parts of the journey.

This Life Recovery Guide includes a special section entitled "Making It Personal" for each of the studies. These are not intended to be group activities. This section provides you with activities and suggestions for implementation of the wisdom found in steps four through nine of the Twelve Steps of Alcoholics Anonymous. These are demanding steps—they call us to a deeper self-awareness and a fundamental change. They will take time.

The experience of God changing us can be the source of new freedom and joy in our daily lives. It is our prayer that you will find healing and hope as you take these steps toward recovery from guilt.

May your roots sink deeply in the soil of God's love.

Juanita and Dale Ryan

1
Facing the Truth About Ourselves

"Before I started this process I didn't know myself at all," Bob said to his Twelve-Step group. "My wife would ask me to talk with her about my thoughts and feelings, or to simply reflect on the events of my day, and I would come up blank. Learning to face the truth was like slowly turning on a light in a very dark room. I have discovered all kinds of things about myself. Some of them are not very pretty. Some of them are encouraging. But the experience of growing self-awareness has been the starting point for real change and growth in my life."

Self-awareness is both frightening and exciting. It is like opening the door to a messy closet. The first thing you see is the mess. But unless we take a look at the mess in our closet, we cannot begin the process of sorting and cleaning. We will discover things about ourselves that we did not know or that we have long forgotten. We will find treasures worth keeping. And we will also find stuff that will need to be discarded.

It is important to remember that as we grow in our capacity for honesty, we will probably experience shame. We may find ourselves feeling that we are irreparably bad. We may say hateful things to ourselves. If you played the role of the scapegoat in your family (the one who was seen as the "problem" or the "black sheep" of the family), looking at your sins and failures may seem to confirm your worst fears—that you really were a bad, problem child. You will need to remind yourself that your sins and failures do not put you in a category apart from everyone else. Your sins put you in the *same* category as everyone else. You are part of the human family of sinners. If the process of working on guilt leads to a dead end, however, we recommend that you talk about these feelings with a pastor, spiritual director, therapist or sponsor.

If you played the role of the compliant child in your family (good, helpful, successful), this step will come with a different set of dangers. Looking at your sins may seem to confirm the terrible fear that no matter how hard you try, you can never be good enough. Fortunately, however, spiritual growth does not come from "trying," or "trying harder," or even "trying your hardest." No matter how hard we try, we are humans who sin and who need God's mercy and forgiveness every day. Taking the steps which lead to forgiveness from guilt may help you to let go of the harsh demands you place on yourself, and allow yourself to rest quietly in God's merciful arms.

☐ Personal Reflection _____

1. What feelings do you have as you approach taking a moral inventory of your life?

2. The fourth step of Alcoholics Anonymous suggests that we undertake a "fearless" inventory of our lives. But we usually start with many fears. What fears do you have?

3. What would give you the courage you need to begin your inventory?

☐ **Bible Study**_____

This is the message we have heard from him and declare to you: God is light; in him there is no darkness at all. If we claim to have fellowship with him yet walk in the darkness, we lie and do not live by the truth. But if we walk in the light, as he is in the light, we have fellowship with one another, and the blood of Jesus, his Son, purifies us from all sin.

If we claim to be without sin, we deceive ourselves and the truth is not in us. If we confess our sins, he is faithful and just and will forgive us our sins and purify us from all unrighteousness. If we claim we have not sinned, we make him out to be a liar and his word has no place in our lives. My dear children, I write this to you so that you will not sin. But if anybody does sin, we have one who speaks to the Father in our defense—Jesus Christ, the Righteous One. He is the atoning sacrifice for our sins, and not only for ours but also for the sins of the whole world. (1 John 1:5—2:2)

1. What insights did you gain from your time of personal reflection?

2. The text begins by stating, "God is light; in him there is no darkness at all." What images does that bring to mind?

What is the significance of God being "light"?

3. What do you think it means to "walk in the darkness"?

4. What do you think it means to "walk in the light"?

5. What are the consequences of honesty according to this text?

6. What are the consequences of dishonesty according to this text?

7. What experiences have you had with these consequences?

8. The last part of this text tells us that Jesus speaks on our behalf and atones for us (repairs our relationship with God) when we sin.

How might this give you greater courage as you make your inventory?

☐ **Prayer** _____

What would you like to say to the God who is light?

☐ **Making It Personal** _____

Doing your inventory. A few general guidelines may help you as you prepare for the truth-telling to which this text calls us. First, a moral inventory should almost always be written. Be as specific as possible and take your time. Work at this over a period of several days or weeks. Be aware of a tendency to put off starting or completing your inventory. It is not reasonable to expect that this will be a pleasant activity. But it is an important one. If you find yourself experiencing a great deal of shame or becoming depressed, seek out a pastor or therapist who can help you be kind to yourself. If you are participating in a Twelve-Step program, your sponsor will be an important resource at this time. Remember it is God who will empower you to make your inventory. Keep in mind that the skills you learn in making a moral inventory will be used over and over again throughout your life. You don't have to do a perfect, exhaustive inventory all at once.

1. Spend some time focusing on the image: "God is light." Let the light of God's loving, healing presence shine into all the parts of your life. God's light is warm and gentle, but it is bright. There is no darkness when God's light is present. Let God's light reveal who you are: your strengths, your weaknesses, your sins, your fears, your gifts. Write freely (without editing or worrying about sentence structure or grammar) whatever thoughts and feelings come to you as a result of God's light shining inside of you. Write without stopping for ten to twenty minutes.

2. Take out one piece of paper for every six years you have lived. Label each page with the appropriate time period (birth-six, seven-twelve, and so on). On each page write whatever memories come to you (you may need more than one page for each time span). Focus on unhealed memories, unresolved feelings, behaviors that were destructive to yourself or someone else, strengths, survival skills and ways you can see that God took care of you. Be as specific with names, dates, events and behaviors as you can.

3. Take out a piece of paper for each category of relationship in your life. Label them appropriately: parents, siblings, spouse, children, friends, coworkers, God and self. What problems do you have in each of these relationships? What destructive, hurtful behaviors are you aware of engaging in toward these people (yourself included)? What are you contributing in these relationships?

4. Write a comprehensive statement about yourself based on the previous three exercises. Begin with these statements, "I am a precious child of God. When the light of God's loving presence shines on my life, this is what I see . . ."

2
Admitting Our Wrongs

"I always kept everything in," Sue began. *"It was like I had two lives.* One that everyone saw, and one that only I knew about. Because of the secrets, I was full of shame and confusion. I expected it to be very painful to admit my wrongs. But, when I finally told everything to another human being, it was very different from what I expected. The person I told was not shocked; she did not shame me; she accepted me and told me she respected my courage and honesty. I felt like I would never be the same. Something changed inside."

Admitting our wrongs is a threefold process of confession. First, we admit our wrongs to God, then we admit our wrongs to ourselves, and then we admit our wrongs to another human being. This process can be a powerful, life-changing experience. We all long to be known; to share the secrets that are so toxic to our souls; to experience the grace of being loved and accepted—sins and all. The spiritual discipline of confession provides the structure within which we can experience this grace in practical ways.

God invites us to the spiritual discipline of confession. "Confess your sins to each other and pray for each other so that you may be healed" (James 5:16). Confession is an act of obedience to this biblical imperative. It is an imperative with a promise of healing. May God grant you the courage you need as you practice the spiritual discipline of confession.

☐ **Personal Reflection** _____

1. What feelings do you have as you approach confession?

2. What internal and external barriers stand in your way as you approach taking this step?

☐ **Bible Study**_____

Have mercy on me, O God,
    according to your unfailing love;
according to your great compassion
    blot out my transgressions.
Wash away all my iniquity
    and cleanse me from my sin.
For I know my transgressions,
    and my sin is always before me.

Surely you desire truth in the inner parts;
    you teach me wisdom in the inmost place. (Psalm 51:1-3, 6)

1. What insights did you gain from your time of personal reflection?

2. How does the psalmist describe God in this text?

3. How does this compare with how you experience God?

4. Restate in your own words what the psalmist asks of God.

5. What do you want to ask of God?

6. The psalmist states, "For I know my transgressions, and my sin is always before me." Having prepared a moral inventory, you have had some experience with an increased awareness of the exact nature of your wrongs. What has it been like for you to be aware, in a focused way, of your wrongs?

7. Use the verbs *wash* and *cleanse* from this text as a focus for reflection. Picture God washing and cleansing you. Spend a few minutes with these images. What thoughts and feelings do you have in response to these images?

☐ **Prayer** _____

What do you want to say to the God whose love is unfailing?

☐ **Making It Personal** _____

Admitting the exact nature of our wrongs. This step has three inter-secting parts: admitting to God, admitting to ourselves, and admit-ting to another human being. It is helpful to begin with admitting to God and to proceed in the order in which these are listed. It is important to base your confession on the inventory made in connec-tion with the previous study. You will need to choose a person to hear your confession. The person should understand the importance and limited goals of this step in the process of recovery from guilt, be able to observe strict confidentiality and be a safe person for you emotionally (nonjudgmental, compassionate and mercy-full).

1. The first admission is to God. Take time to do this in an unhurried way. If you find yourself hesitant to approach God, pay attention to your images of God. Begin by admitting to God that your images are distorted. Spend some time focusing, as the psalmist did, on God's unfailing love and great compassion for you. Read the moral inven-tory you have prepared aloud to God. Read a small section at a time. Take time to be silent before God. End this time by rereading the texts from the first study and from this study. Thank God for being forgiving and merciful.

2. The second admission is to yourself. This may seem redundant but it is not. The admission to ourselves is important for two reasons. First, admitting our wrongs to ourselves means that we are no longer deceiving ourselves. This admission involves embracing parts of ourselves that we have rejected. It involves a complex process of integrating what some have called the *shadow* parts of ourselves into our self-understanding. Second, admitting our wrongs to ourselves means that we need to show mercy to ourselves. We need to stop demanding perfection and face our human failings with the same compassion for ourselves that God extends toward us. Read your inventory aloud a second time, this time to yourself. Listen to your words as if you were listening with compassion to a friend you love. Respond with words of affirmation. It may even be helpful to write a letter to yourself, acknowledging that you have heard the admissions and extend mercy and forgiveness toward yourself.

During the admission to God and to yourself, you may have remembered more items that you want to include in your inventory. If so, write them down.

3. The third admission is to another human being. We suggest clarifying with the person whom you have chosen to listen to your confession that your expectation of them is that they will listen. It is not their task to examine, clarify, educate, evaluate, or speak on God's behalf. If you wish to do so, ask the person who has heard your inventory for simple feedback. But do not expect them to absolve you of all your guilt—this is just one step in the process of recovery from guilt; you are not done yet. It may be helpful, however, if the person hearing your inventory is able to affirm your courage and to reassure you that God honors your honesty. Reading your inventory to another person will not be the first time for you to hear your inventory read aloud. You have already read it twice—to God and to yourself. As you read, however, additional memories may return, so allow time to write these down. Do not hold back from talking about whatever is pressing inside of you.

3
Getting Ready
for Change

"I have been this way all my life," John said. *"I have always isolated* myself, and procrastinated, and talked to myself in harsh, critical ways. You would think I would be ready at a moment's notice to have God remove these defects. But I am not. I'm not sure what holds me back. I guess the way I am is the only way I know how to be. I remember once we bought my son a pair of new tennis shoes which he wore for the first time to preschool. He looked up at me that day and said, 'My friends won't recognize me with my new shoes on.' Maybe that is how I feel. How will I recognize myself if these really basic things change? Who will I be without my defects?"

Defects of character are patterns of behavior that we have developed to protect and defend ourselves. Often they are patterns which allowed us to survive the difficult environments we experienced as children. Letting go of character defects can, therefore, feel like a threat to our survival.

For this reason, the process of becoming "entirely ready to have God remove all of our defects of character" will involve us in a major struggle. It will be helpful to anticipate some of what we might experience in this battle. Some defects, for example, will be more difficult to let go of than others. And letting go of any of our defects will involve us in grief work because we will experience their removal as a loss. It's also reasonable to expect that we will resist these changes at the same time that we want and seek them.

May God help you to focus on the healing and freedom that will come as God begins to remove your defects of character.

☐ Personal Reflection ————————————————————————

1. What changes are you aware of wanting in your life?

2. What gains would you experience if you made these changes?

☐ Bible Study————————————————————————————

Blessed is he
    whose transgressions are forgiven,
    whose sins are covered.
Blessed is the man
    whose sin the LORD does not count against him
    and in whose spirit is no deceit.

When I kept silent,
    my bones wasted away
    through my groaning all day long.
For day and night
    your hand was heavy upon me;
my strength was sapped

as in the heat of summer.
Then I acknowledged my sin to you
  and did not cover up my iniquity.
I said, "I will confess
  my transgressions to the LORD"—
and you forgave
  the guilt of my sin.

Therefore let everyone who is godly pray to you
  while you may be found;
surely when the mighty waters rise,
  they will not reach him.
You are my hiding place;
  you will protect me from trouble
  and surround me with songs of deliverance.

I will instruct you and teach you in the way you should go;
  I will counsel you and watch over you.
Do not be like the horse or the mule,
  which have no understanding
but must be controlled by bit and bridle
  or they will not come to you.
Many are the woes of the wicked,
  but the LORD's unfailing love
  surrounds the man who trusts in him.

Rejoice in the LORD and be glad, you righteous;
  sing, all you who are upright in heart! (Psalm 32)

---

1. What insights did you gain from your time of personal reflection?

2. Restate in your own words what the psalmist experienced when he kept silent about his sin.

3. Restate in your own words what the psalmist experienced when he acknowledged his sin.

4. What might cause people to be silent and deceitful about their sin?

5. What does this text tell us about what God does for us?

6. What advice does the psalmist give us from his own experience?

7. What thoughts and feelings do you have in response to the advice the psalmist offers?

8. What experiences have you had with covering your sins?

with confessing your sins?

☐ Prayer _____

What would you like to say to the God who surrounds you with songs of deliverance?

☐ Making It Personal _____

Becoming ready to have God remove all our defects of character. Becoming "entirely ready" is often a major obstacle for perfectionists. What is important is to start wherever you are. It's a mistake to try to fake readiness or willingness. It is not reasonable to expect yourself to become totally ready at the beginning of this process. Take whatever time you need. Don't make the mistake of skipping past this step because it does not seem as action-oriented as some of the other steps.

1. In order to become ready to have God remove our defects of character we need to be aware of what these defects are. List the defects of character that you have recognized as a result of your work up to this point.

2. In order to become ready for God to remove our defects of character we need to explore our relationship with God. Describe the images of God which come to mind when you think about God removing your defects. (Do you see God as gentle, loving, wise and wanting to bring you joy, or do you see God as punitive, arbitrary and abusive?) Meditate again on the images of God found in the text for this study.

3. In order to become ready for God to remove our defects of character we need to grieve the losses which will come from these changes. Describe how your defects of character have protected you. Identify losses you may experience if you let God remove your defects. Describe the feelings you have about the anticipation of these losses.

4. In order to become ready for God to remove our defects of character we need God's help. Review the first three steps of Alcoholics Anonymous (they are reprinted on pp. 52-53) in this context, and then write a prayer asking God to help you become entirely ready to have all your defects of character removed.

4
Asking God to Change Us

"*I can hardly believe how fiercely I hung on to my dysfunctions,*" said Peter. "It has been a major-league battle to let go. I am beginning, however, to see the changes. God is beginning to remove my defects. Fortunately, God is a gentle, patient physician who knows I can only tolerate a little change at a time. But every little bit of change I experience makes me want more."

As we humbly ask God to remove our shortcomings, it is important to remember that "humbly asking" does not require us to shame ourselves. Humility is the ability to admit basic truths: we cannot do this in our own power; we need God's help; we acknowledge our shortcomings and the destructive role they have in our lives, and we ask God to help us change.

We have practiced our defects and shortcomings for a long time. They have protected us for many years from painful realities about ourselves and our experiences. God knows that we are capable of change and that lasting change takes time. God is ready to pull the weeds from our gardens and to plant flowers. It is our task to humbly ask that God do this work in us.

☐ Personal Reflection _____

1. Which of your shortcomings would you be especially relieved to have God remove? Explain.

2. Which of your shortcomings are you especially reluctant to give up? Explain.

☐ Bible Study_____

Cleanse me with hyssop, and I will be clean;
  wash me, and I will be whiter than snow.
Let me hear joy and gladness;
  let the bones you have crushed rejoice.
Hide your face from my sins
  and blot out all my iniquity.

Create in me a pure heart, O God,
  and renew a steadfast spirit within me.
Do not cast me from your presence
  or take your Holy Spirit from me.
Restore to me the joy of your salvation
  and grant me a willing spirit, to sustain me.

Then I will teach transgressors your ways,
  and sinners will turn back to you.
Save me from bloodguilt, O God,
  the God who saves me,

and my tongue will sing of your righteousness.
O Lord, open my lips,
    and my mouth will declare your praise.
You do not delight in sacrifice, or I would bring it;
    you do not take pleasure in burnt offerings.
The sacrifices of God are a broken spirit;
    a broken and contrite heart,
      O God, you will not despise. (Psalm 51:7-17)

---

1. What insights did you gain from your time of personal reflection?

2. In the second study, we looked at the first half of this psalm in which the writer confesses his sin to God. The psalmist is now asking for God's response. What does he ask God to do in response to his failures?

3. Restate in your own words the changes in character which the psalmist seeks.

4. What response does the psalmist anticipate?

What does he expect to experience when God responds?

5. The text ends by saying that what we need for these changes to take place is a broken and contrite heart. What is a "broken and contrite" heart?

6. Why is it important to have a "broken and contrite" heart?

7. Of the requests which the psalmist makes of God, which are the most applicable to your situation?

8. Picture God restoring joy to you. What images come to mind?

What response do you have to these images?

☐ **Prayer** _____

What would you like to humbly ask of God at this time?

☐ **Making It Personal** _____

Humbly asking God to remove our shortcomings. Our shortcomings have been with us for a long time. It will take time for God to remove them. It will require patience and persistence on our part. It will require us to grieve the loss of our old ways. At this stage in the journey it may be particularly important to seek support from a support group and/or a counselor. It is not God's intentions for us to be alone with these struggles.

1. Begin by reviewing the list of character defects or shortcomings that emerged from your prior work. Is there anything that you would add to your inventory at this time?

2. After each shortcoming you have identified write its opposite. The goal of this exercise is to identify the qualities of character that God will be bringing about in our lives. For example:

Shortcoming: I isolate myself from people.

Anticipated change: I will become more trusting and will reach out in appropriate ways to other people.

3. Spend some time being aware of yourself as one of God's needy children. Journal about whatever feelings you have about God at this time. Ask for God's help in whatever healing you need.

4. Ask God to remove each of the wrongs, defects of character and shortcomings you have identified in your inventory. Talk to God about your fears and hopes, your grief and joy.

5. Thank God for working in you to change you from the inside out.

5
Becoming Willing to Make Amends

"I guess I have spent a lot of time and energy blaming everyone else for my addiction," Molly said. "Blaming has been one of my primary defenses. It has protected me from taking a look at myself. It is a good thing that I was able to see this as one of my shortcomings and that God has been changing me. Otherwise, I do not know how I would have faced the fact that I have harmed other people. When I first started to think about making amends, I came up blank. My first response was my old predictable reaction: 'I'm the one who has been harmed!' But as I asked for God's help, God began to show me more than I wanted to see. I have been hurt by others. But I have also hurt others. It is time for me to face this other half of reality."

Our compulsions and addictions helped us to soothe our pain. But they also created a great deal of destruction in our own lives and in the lives of other people. We have harmed other people. It is time to face this truth. The point of facing this reality is not to crawl into a dark hole in the ground for the rest of our lives. The point is just the opposite. This is our opportunity to repair the relational bridges that have been damaged so that we can enjoy restored relationships with others.

☐ **Personal Reflection** _____

1. What are your primary feelings as you think about making amends?

2. What might be standing in your way of becoming willing to make amends?

☐ **Bible Study** _____

Who is wise and understanding among you? Let him show it by his good life, by deeds done in the humility that comes from wisdom. But if you harbor bitter envy and selfish ambition in your hearts, do not boast about it or deny the truth. Such "wisdom" does not come down from heaven but is earthly, unspiritual, of the devil. For where you have envy and selfish ambition, there you find disorder and every evil practice.

But the wisdom that comes from heaven is first of all pure; then peace-loving, considerate, submissive, full of mercy and good fruit, impartial and sincere. (James 3:13-17)

1. What insights did you gain from your time of personal reflection?

2. This text makes a connection between an internal state characterized by wisdom and understanding and an external reality of "deeds done in humility." How are these related?

3. What experiences have you had with the relationship between wisdom and humble deeds?

4. The text also tells us that there is a relationship between the experience of "bitter envy" and "selfish ambition" and behaviors characterized by "disorder and every evil practice." What relationship do you see between these experiences and behaviors?

5. What experiences have you had with shame-based comparisons leading to disorder and evil practice?

6. If we find ourselves harboring bitter envy and selfish ambition, the writer advises us, "Do not boast about it or deny the truth." Letting go of denial and telling the truth are powerful antidotes for these poisons. Why is this?

7. What experiences have you had with the effect on honesty on bitterness and selfish ambition?

8. The text lists characteristics of the wisdom that comes from heaven. Which of these characteristics are you aware of in your own life?

Which of these characteristics would you like God to strengthen in you as you work on becoming willing to make amends?

☐ **Prayer** _____

What wisdom would you like to ask from God?

☐ **Making It Personal** _____

Making a list of persons harmed and becoming willing to make amends. The moral inventory you have made will provide the information you need to make a list of people you have harmed. We can harm with words, harm financially, harm physically, harm by gossiping, harm by judging. We can also harm the people closest to us by neglecting them. The list of people we have harmed through neglect will include those who had a rightful claim on our attention (for example, children, spouses and close friends). It is important to remember that this is not a list of people you need to placate—or a list of the people you need to change—or a list of the people you must try to please. It is a list of people you have harmed. Also, remember that putting someone's name on the list does not necessarily mean that you will make amends to them. Try to focus for now on making a comprehensive list of people you have harmed—in the next study we will work on what practical things can be done with this information.

1. Ask God to give you the wisdom, courage and recall you need to make your list.

2. Make a list with names, dates and specific information about the harm done.

3. Go over each name on the list. Write down whatever feelings you have about this person at this time.

4. If you are angry with this person you may not be ready to make amends. Talk to God about your anger, fear and hurt.

5. Ask God to show you what barriers might stand in the way of being ready to make amends to each person. Write down whatever thoughts you have.

6. Ask God to heal you and free you so you can become willing to make amends.

6
Making Amends

"I was so frightened when I called Susan," said Beth. *"I hadn't talked* to her for five years. We used to be best friends. But she was deeply hurt by the things I said and did when I was actively abusing alcohol. So much so that she didn't invite me to her wedding two years ago. I was afraid she would slam the phone in my ear. But when I told her I was working on making amends, she seemed to know what I was talking about. I asked to meet her for coffee so I could make amends for the hurtful things I had said. We met. She listened. I said everything I had prepared to say. And then we talked for two hours. I got my friend back! That surprised me. I had been so afraid and ashamed that I had put the call off for months. Years, really. I am so glad that I didn't put it off forever."

Making amends may seem like an impossible step to take. It does demand a great deal of us. But, as in all of the steps of spiritual growth, we receive back more than we give. It is important to recognize that we will not always be rewarded with restored relationships. Our task is to make amends, not to anticipate how others will respond. But sometimes broken relationships can experience healing. Regardless of how people respond, it is a rich reward to experience the serenity that comes from saying, "I blew it. I harmed you. I am sorry." Making amends can lead to spiritual growth, whether or not the process has any effect on others.

Each new step of spiritual growth requires us to return to the fundamentals of the spiritual life. We need to remember that we are powerless but that God is powerful. The practical effect of these truths will become clear as we rely on God to help us make amends to those we have harmed.

☐ **Personal Reflection** _____

1. What feelings do you have as you prepare to make amends?

2. What personal benefit do you anticipate from the spiritual discipline of making amends?

☐ **Bible Study** _____

Therefore, if you are offering your gift at the altar and there remember that your brother has something against you, leave your gift, there in front of the altar. First go and be reconciled to your brother; then come and offer your gift.

You have heard that it was said, "Love your neighbor and hate your enemy." But I tell you: Love your enemies and pray for those who persecute you, that you may be sons of your Father in heaven. He causes his sun to rise on the evil and the good, and sends rain on the righteous and the unrighteous. (Matthew 5: 23-24, 43-45)

1. What insights did you gain from your time of personal reflection?

2. What does this text tell us about God?

3. What does the text tell us about how God wants us to relate to others?

4. The text tells us that making amends is a prerequisite to community worship. What thoughts and feelings do you have about this?

5. Why do you think making amends is such an important spiritual discipline?

6. Making amends is presented as an ordinary, normal part of life. How might this thought help you as you take this step?

7. What experiences have you had with actively seeking reconciliation with another person?

8. What struggles have you had with loving your enemies?

☐ **Prayer** _____

What would you like to say to God as you prepare to make amends?

☐ **Making It Personal** _____

Making amends. For most of us, the process of deciding how to make amends is complicated. We strongly recommend consultation with a pastor or therapist before seeking to make amends in situations involving abuse, broken relationships, violence or other trauma. Making direct amends is not always possible. Ask God for wisdom in knowing how to reach people, knowing the right timing, and being ready. If a person is unavailable, it is sometimes helpful to make indirect amends by offering appropriate gifts of kindness to a third party. Making amends can sometimes injure other people. An example of this would be if you had an affair with someone and their spouse did not know about it. To make amends to that person or to the spouse may be injurious to their relationship. We need to ask for wisdom to know when this "injury exception" applies. Be aware of a tendency to avoid making the amends that you clearly need to make.
1. Amends are primarily communications. You may call, write or meet with a person. Face-to-face meetings are the most powerful if they are possible.

2. Be simple and specific in describing to the other person what you have done to harm them.

3. Keep the focus on your part of the problem. Do not focus on their contribution to the problem. If they want to talk about their part, that is okay. But you need to stay focused on your harmful behaviors.

4. Do not expect a response. Do not ask them to say, "I forgive you."

5. Ask "What can I do to make it right?" If you have harmed them financially, you will need to set up a plan to pay them back. If you have neglected a spouse for several years, you may want to set up a plan to give them a gift of your time. Sometimes the best amend we can make is to change our harmful behavior. Sometimes an acknowledgment of our behavior and the harm it caused may be all the amends we are able to make.

6. When you are finished with what you have prepared to say, thank the person for listening to you and listen to any response they may wish to make.

7. Remember that making amends is a part of the process of recovery from guilt. It is not the end of the process. We strongly encourage you to continue to learn from working the Twelve-Step process until these tools become a part of your daily life. Steps ten, eleven and twelve of the Twelve Steps of Alcoholics Anonymous focus on the skills needed to integrate this process into daily life. For an introduction to the biblical basis of these steps we encourage you to work through the Life Recovery Guide entitled *Recovery: A Lifelong Journey,* which examines these steps.

Leader's Notes

You may be experiencing a variety of feelings as you anticipate leading a group using a Life Recovery Guide. You may feel inadequate for the task and afraid of what will happen. If this is the case, know you are in good company. Many of the kings, prophets and apostles in the Bible felt inadequate and afraid. Many other small group leaders share this experience of fear as well.

Your willingness to lead, however, is a gift to the other group members. It might help if you tell them about your feelings and ask them to pray for you. Keep in mind that the other group members share the responsibility for the group. And realize that it is God's work to bring insight, comfort, healing and recovery to group members. Your role is simply to provide guidance to the discussion. The suggestions listed below will help you to provide that guidance.

Using the Life Recovery Guides

This Life Recovery Guide is one in a series of guides. The series was designed to be a flexible tool that can be used in various combinations by individuals and groups—such as support groups, Bible studies and Sunday-school classes. All of the guides in this series are designed to be useful to anyone. Each guide has a specific focus, but all are written with a general audience in mind.

Many congregation-based recovery ministries use the Life Recovery Guides as part of the curriculum for "newcomers" groups. It can be a critical step in the recovery process to recognize that "recovery" is not a new set of ideas or the latest trend in popular psychology. Finding that the Bible is attentive to our struggles can often provide the courage needed to continue when the journey becomes painful.

We strongly recommend that careful attention be given to the group dynamics of the Bible study. Traditional Bible studies in the Christian community tend to be cognitively oriented, leadership tends to be well defined, commenting on statements by other participants is usually encouraged, giving advice is often valued, and sharing concerns expressed in the group with nonparticipants is often understood to be a kind of caring. Special attention will often be needed, therefore, to use the Life Recovery Guides in a way that teaches group participants the norms, values and group dynamics of the support group ministry to which the person is being introduced.

For example, if the Life Recovery Guides are used as an introductory experience that leads toward participation in a Twelve-Step group, then the group dynamics should probably resemble as much as possible those of a Twelve-Step group. Group facilitators should take time to carefully explain the purpose of the group and to introduce group participants to new group norms. It will probably take some time and practice, for example, to assimilate the concept of "cross talk." Groups using the Life Recovery Guides can help build a biblical foundation for what follows in the recovery process. But they can also help people to develop the skills needed to benefit from a support group experience.

Each guide contains six studies. If eight guides are used, they can provide a year-long curriculum series. Or if the guides are used in pairs, they can provide studies for a quarter (twelve weeks). The following are some ways that you might find it helpful to use the guides in combination with one another:

Topic	Number of Studies/Weeks	Guides to Use
Introduction to Recovery	12	Recovery from Distorted Images of God
		Recovery from Distorted Images of Self
Abuse	30	Recovery from Abuse
		Recovery from Shame
		Recovery from Distorted Images of Self
		Recovery from Fear
		Recovery from Spiritual Abuse
Addictions	30	Recovery from Addictions (Steps 1-3)
		Recovery from Guilt (Steps 4-9)
		Recovery: A Lifelong Journey (Steps 10-12)
		Recovery from Codependency
		Recovery from Workaholism
Family Dysfunctions	18	Recovery from Family Dysfunctions
		Recovery from Distorted Images of God
		Recovery from Distorted Images of Self
Divorce	30	Recovery from Depression
		Recovery from Loss
		Recovery from Shame
		Recovery from Broken Relationships
		Recovery from Bitterness
Grief and Loss	24	Recovery from Loss
		Recovery from Fear
		Recovery from Depression
		Recovery from Distorted Images of God

Preparing to Lead

1. Develop realistic expectations of yourself as a small group leader. Do not feel that you have to "have it all together." Rather, commit yourself to an ongoing discipline of honesty about your own needs. As you grow in honesty about your own needs, you will grow as well in your capacity for compassion, gentleness and patience with yourself and with others. As a leader, you can encourage an atmosphere of honesty by being honest about yourself.

2. Pray. Pray for yourself and your own recovery. Pray for the group members. Invite the Holy Spirit to be present as you prepare and as you meet.

3. Read the study several times.

4. Take your time to thoughtfully work through each question, writing out your answers.

5. After completing your personal study, read through the leader's notes for the study you are leading. These notes are designed to help you in several ways. First, they tell you the purpose the authors had in mind while writing the study. Take time to think through how the questions work together to accomplish that purpose. Second, the notes provide you with additional background information or comments on some of the questions. This information can be useful if people have difficulty understanding or answering a question. Third, the leader's notes can alert you to potential problems you may encounter during the study.

6. If you wish to remind yourself during the group discussion of anything mentioned in the leader's notes, make a note to yourself below that question in your study guide.

Leading the Study

1. Begin on time. You may want to open in prayer, or have a group member do so.

2. Be sure everyone has a study guide. Decide as a group if you want people to do the study on their own ahead of time. If your time together is limited, it will be helpful for people to prepare in advance.

3. At the beginning of your first time together, explain that these studies are meant to be discussions, not lectures. Encourage the members of the group to participate. However, do not put pressure on those who may be hesitant to speak during the first few sessions. Clearly state that people do not need to share anything they

do not feel safe sharing. Remind people that it will take time to trust each other.

4. Read aloud the group guidelines listed in the front of the guide. These commitments are important in creating a safe place for people to talk and trust and feel.

5. The covers of the Life Recovery Guides are designed to incorporate both symbols of the past and hope for the future. During your first meeting, allow the group to describe what they see in the cover and respond to it.

6. Read aloud the introductory paragraphs at the beginning of the discussion for the day. This will orient the group to the passage being studied.

7. The personal reflection questions are designed to help group members focus on some aspect of their experience. Hopefully, they will help group members to be more aware of the frame of reference and life experience which they bring to the study. The personal reflection section can be done prior to the group meeting or as the first part of the meeting. If the group does not prepare in advance, approximately ten minutes will be needed for individuals to consider these questions.

The personal reflection questions are not designed to be used directly for group discussion. Rather, the first question in the Bible study section is intended to give group members an opportunity to reveal what they feel safe sharing from their time of personal reflection.

8. Read the passage aloud. You may choose to do this yourself, or prior to the study you might ask someone else to read.

9. As you begin to ask the questions in the guide, keep several things in mind. First, the questions are designed to be used just as they are written. If you wish, you may simply read them aloud to the group. Or you may prefer to express them in your own words. However, unnecessary rewording of the questions is not recommended.

Second, the questions are intended to guide the group toward understanding and applying the main idea of the study. You will find the purpose of each study described in the leader's notes. You should try to understand how the study questions and the biblical text work together to lead the group in that direction.

There may be times when it is appropriate to deviate from the study guide. For example, a question may have already been answered. If so, move on to the next question. Or someone may raise an important question not covered in the guide. Take time to discuss it! The important thing is to use discretion. There may be many routes you can travel to reach the goal of the study. But the easiest route is usually the one we have suggested.

10. Don't be afraid of silence. People need time to think about the question before formulating their answers.

11. Draw out a variety of responses from the group. Ask, "Who else has some thoughts about this?" or "How did some of the rest of you respond?" until several people have given answers to the question.

12. Acknowledge all contributions. Try to be affirming whenever possible. Never reject an answer. If it seems clearly wrong to you, ask, "Which part of the text led you to that conclusion?" or "What do the rest of you think?"

13. Realize that not every answer will be addressed to you, even though this will probably happen at first. As group members become more at ease, they will begin to interact more effectively with each other. This is a sign of a healthy discussion.

14. Don't be afraid of controversy. It can be very stimulating. Differences can enrich our lives. If you don't resolve an issue completely, don't be frustrated. Move on and keep it in mind for later. A subsequent study may resolve the problem. Or, the issue may not be resolved—not all questions have answers!

15. Stick to the passage under consideration. It should be the source for answering the questions. Discourage the group from unnecessary cross-referencing. Likewise, stick to the subject and avoid going off on tangents.

16. Periodically summarize what the group has said about the topic.

This helps to draw together the various ideas mentioned and gives continuity to the study. But be careful not to use summary statements as an opportunity to give a sermon!

17. During the discussion, feel free to share your own responses. Your honesty about your own recovery can set a tone for the group to feel safe in sharing. Be careful not to dominate the time, but do allow time for your own needs as a group member.

18. Each study ends with a time for prayer. There are several ways to handle this time in a group. The person who leads each study could lead the group in a prayer or you could allow time for group participation. Remember that some members of your group may feel uncomfortable about participating in public prayer. It might be helpful to discuss this with the group during your first meeting and to reach some agreement about how to proceed.

19. Realize that trust in a group grows over time. During the first couple meetings, people will be assessing how safe they will feel in the group. Do not be discouraged if people share only superficially at first. The level of trust will grow slowly but steadily.

Listening to Emotional Pain

Life Recovery Guides are designed to take seriously the pain and struggle that is part of life. People will experience a variety of emotions during these studies. Your role as group leader is not to act as a professional counselor. Instead it is to be a friend who listens to emotional pain. Listening is a gift you can give to hurting people. For many, it is not an easy gift to give. The following suggestions can help you listen more effectively to people in emotional pain.

1. Remember that you are not responsible to take the pain away. People in helping relationships often feel that they are being asked to make the other person feel better. This is usually related to the helper's own patterns of not being comfortable with painful feelings.

2. Not only are you not responsible to take the pain away, one of the things people need most is an opportunity to face and to experience the pain in their lives. They have usually spent years denying their pain and running from it. Healing can come when we are able to face our pain in the presence of someone who cares about us. Rather than trying to take the pain away, commit yourself to listening attentively as it is expressed.

3. Realize that some group members may not feel comfortable with expressions of sadness or anger. You may want to acknowledge that such emotions are uncomfortable, but remind the group that part of recovery is to learn to feel and to allow others to feel.

4. Be very cautious about giving answers and advice. Advice and answers may make you feel better or feel competent, but they may also minimize people's problems and their painful feelings. Simple solutions rarely work, and they can easily communicate "You should be better now" or "You shouldn't really be talking about this."

5. Be sure to communicate direct affirmation any time people talk about their painful emotions. It takes courage to talk about our pain because it creates anxiety for us. It is a great gift to be trusted by those who are struggling.

The Twelve Steps of Alcoholics Anonymous

   1. We admitted we were powerless over alcohol—that our lives had become unmanageable.

   2. Came to believe that a Power greater than ourselves could restore us to sanity.

   3. Made a decision to turn our will and our lives over to the care of God as we understood Him.

   4. Made a searching and fearless moral inventory of ourselves.

   5. Admitted to God, to ourselves, and to another human being the exact nature of our wrongs.

   6. Were entirely ready to have God remove all these defects of character.

   7. Humbly asked Him to remove our shortcomings.

   8. Made a list of all persons we had harmed, and became willing to make amends to them all.

9. Made direct amends to such people wherever possible, except when to do so would injure them or others.

10. Continued to take personal inventory and when we were wrong promptly admitted it.

11. Sought through prayer and meditation to improve our conscious contact with God as we understood Him, praying only for knowledge of His will for us and the power to carry that out.

12. Having had a spiritual awakening as the result of these steps, we tried to carry this message to alcoholics, and to practice these principles in all our affairs.

See copyright page for Twelve Step credit line.

The following notes refer to the questions in the Bible study portion of each study:

Study 1. Facing the Truth About Ourselves. 1 John 1:5—2:2.

Purpose: To practice facing the truth about our lives.

Question 2. Some people may experience an overwhelming sense of condemnation at the thought that God is light. If God's purpose is to condemn, then to be illumined by God is to be prepared for judgment—to be found out, to be "caught." It may feel like God's searchlight is so sharply focused on me as a guilty person that the light hurts my skin. But God's purpose is not to condemn. Light does give clarity, and we need it to see our failures clearly. But light also helps people who are lost in the dark to find their way.

Question 3. Notice that the text connects "walking in the darkness" with dishonesty, claiming to be without sin, self-deceit (denial), not having "truth" in us and false claims of spiritual maturity. Walking in the light, by contrast, has to do with "living by the truth."

Question 5. The consequences of honesty according to this text include: we will have fellowship with one another and the blood of Jesus will purify us from all sin.

Question 6. The consequences of dishonesty according to this text include self-deceit, making God out to be a liar and disregarding his Word for our lives. People unfamiliar with the culture of the New Testament may have difficulty with the expression "blood of Jesus." Rather than getting distracted with discussions on the relevance of sacrificial understandings of atonement, we encourage you to focus on the goal stated in the text of "purification" from sins. The text says that "being in the light" leads to purity. The point of the text is not so much the "mechanism" of atonement as it is the practical consequences of truthtelling.

Study 2. Admitting Our Wrongs. Psalm 51:1-3, 6.

Purpose: To practice the spiritual discipline of confession.

Question 2. God is described as unfailing in love and great in compassion. God is also described as One who desires truth in the inner parts.

Question 3. Many people who have experienced parents as abusive or abandoning will see God as harsh, punitive and vindictive rather than loving and compassionate. These people will have increased difficulty admitting to God, to themselves and to another human being the exact nature of their wrongs. It is important to focus on the image of God as loving and compassionate in this text.

Question 4. The psalmist asks God to have mercy on him, to blot out his transgression, to wash away his sin, to cleanse him and to teach him wisdom in the inmost place.

Study 3. Getting Ready for Change. Psalm 32.

Purpose: To become ready for God to change us.

Question 2. He experienced sensations of physical exhaustion, perhaps even illness, and deep emotional distress. (Bones wasted, strength sapped, groaning all day long.)

Question 3. He experienced forgiveness, a safe hiding place, protection, instruction, rejoicing and singing.

Question 4. Denial has a thousand faces. We all struggle to tell the truth. But deceit comes easily. You can probably think of many reasons for this deceit. For example, we keep silence because we are afraid. We are deceitful because we don't want to hurt others. We want to avoid punishment. We want to avoid rejection. We want to be "nice" people. We are so accustomed to what is false that we don't remember how to tell the truth.

Question 5. The text is clear that God is a forgiving God. God is a hiding place. God protects when we are in trouble. God teaches us and guides us. God counsels us and watches over us.

Question 6. The psalmist suggests that we pray to God, that we ask for help and forgiveness, that we not be stubborn like a mule, that we rejoice and sing.

Study 4. Asking God to Change Us. Psalm 51:7-17.

Purpose: To seek God's help in the recovery process.

Question 2. The psalmist asks God to wash him and cleanse him, to heal him from the physical consequences of his sin, to remove his sin, not to look at his sin, to save him, not to reject him or leave him because of his sin.

Question 3. The psalmist asks God to give him a pure heart, a steadfast spirit, and a willing spirit that will sustain him. He asks that his joy be restored and that he be helped to express his gratitude to God.

Question 4. The psalmist clearly trusts God's desire and power to respond to all of these requests. When they are granted, he anticipates being able to teach others what he has learned and to express his praise and gratitude.

Question 5. A broken and contrite heart indicates that a person takes his or her wrongdoing seriously, that it causes him sorrow, that she is not blaming or explaining it away but taking appropriate responsibility for her actions. It is a picture of humility before God.

Question 6. A broken and contrite heart is important in a fundamental way. We cannot heal until we know we are ill. We cannot change until we know we have a problem. Blaming others or focusing only on the problems others have caused us does not help us to grow in character. A broken and contrite heart is the beginning of all healing and change. Without it we will only continue on our destructive paths.

Study 5. Becoming Willing to Make Amends. James 3:13-17.

Purpose: To become willing to make amends.

Question 2. Wisdom and understanding allow a person to see reality broadly and deeply. When we have wisdom and understanding, we see our limits and needs. We see the needs and limits of others. We are compassionate toward ourselves and others, and we are able to act on this basis.

Question 4. Bitter envy and selfish ambition are varieties of shame-based comparisons with others. We compare ourselves with others and feel we are not valuable unless we are somehow better than others. It is not enough to be ourselves. So we strive to prove ourselves. We walk over others. We do harm to others, driven by shame to be better-than or more-than others.

Question 6. Shame-based comparisons are always rooted in denial. No one is really "better" or "worse" than me. We are all equally God's precious children. If we pursue the truth we always come back to this point—it is God's love for us that makes us real, not our performance, our effort, our successes, our maturity, our sincerity, our character. We are loved and precious because God loves us and values us. This truth undercuts the foundations of envy and selfish ambition. We do not need to compare ourselves with others—favorably or unfavorably—because the only comparison that counts is God's. And God says, "You are my precious child, I love you."

Study 6. Making Amends. Matthew 5:23-24, 43-45.

Purpose: To practice the spiritual discipline of making amends.

Question 2. God provides and cares for the just and the unjust.

Question 3. We are to actively work on our relationships with others. We are to take responsibility for our wrongdoing. We are to seek to put things right. We are to learn to love and pray for our enemies. It should be emphasized that "to love" does not mean "to like" or "to tolerate abuse" or "to deny our anger." To love a person is to seek what is in their best interests—not necessarily to seek what they think is in their best interests. Ultimately, we pray for our enemies because prayer is a turning over to God of our concerns. When we pray, we seek the best interest of our enemies by turning them over to God

Question 4. The text clearly suggests that making amends has a logical priority over public worship in the spiritual life of the Christian. This emphasis is reminiscent of the prophetic wisdom of the Old Testament. Isaiah made the same point when he found people fasting but not making amends to exploited workers ("On the day of your fasting, you do as you please and exploit all your workers" [Isaiah 58:3]). Making amends is an urgent concern because we are the kind of people who are susceptible to ignoring the fundamentals of godly living while continuing with the external trappings of the religious life. Unlike many other spiritual disciplines, making amends cannot be done as a "performance." Making amends makes a fundamental change in how we relate to others. It is this fundamentally changed life that makes it possible for us to come to worship with honesty before God.

Question 5. It is important to remember that making amends is not just to meet the needs of the person we have wronged. We are called to make amends because it is part of the process of releasing us from the guilt which saps our spiritual strength. We make amends because we need to make amends.

Question 6. Because making amends is a spiritual discipline which is rarely encouraged (much less practiced) in many Christian traditions, it may be difficult for some people to think of it as an "ordinary, normal part of life." It may feel like something that only really "sick" or really "bad" people need to do. It is not, however, presented in the

Bible as an exceptional strategy for only the most difficult cases. It is the normal stuff of the normal Christian life. To be an amend-making person is to be on the Christian path.

For more information about Christian resources for people in recovery and subscription information for STEPS, *the newsletter of the National Association for Christian Recovery, we invite you to write to:*

The National Association for Christian Recovery
P.O. Box 11095
Whittier, California 90603

LIFE RECOVERY GUIDES FROM INTER-VARSITY PRESS
By Dale and Juanita Ryan

Recovery from Abuse. Does the nightmare of abuse ever end? After emotional, verbal and/
or physical abuse how can you develop secure relationships? Recovery is difficult but possible.
This guide will help you turn to God as you put the broken pieces of your life back together
again. Six studies, 64 pages, 1158-3.

Recovery from Addictions. Addictions have always been part of the human predicament.
Chemicals, food, people, sex, work, spending, gambling, religious practices and more can en-
slave us. This guide will help you find the wholeness and restoration that God offers to those
who are struggling with addictions. Six studies, 64 pages, 1155-9.

Recovery from Bitterness. Sometimes forgiveness gets blocked, stuck, restrained and entangled. We find our hearts turning toward bitterness and revenge. Our inability to forgive
can make us feel like spiritual failures. This guide will help us find the strength to change
bitterness into forgiveness. Six studies, 64 pages, 1154-0.

Recovery from Broken Relationships. Divorce. Family conflict. Death. We may learn to fear
closeness because we don't want to experience another separation from someone we love. God
wants to heal us of the pain of lost relationships. These studies help us discover how to risk
love again and build healthy relationships that will endure. Six studies, 64 pages, 1165-6.

Recovery from Codependency. The fear, anger and helplessness people feel when someone
they love is addicted can lead to desperate attempts to take care of, or control, the loved one.
Both the addicted person's behavior and the frenzied codependent behavior progress in a
destructive downward spiral of denial and blame. This guide will help you to let go of over-
responsibility and entrust the people you love to God. Six studies, 64 pages, 1156-7.

Recovery from Depression. From time to time we all experience feelings of hopelessness
in response to difficult events in life—broken relationships, death, unemployment and so on.
Sometimes we are not able to work through those feelings alone. And we need to be pointed
toward the source of hope. This guide will show you the way. Six studies, 64 pages, 1161-3.

Recovery from Distorted Images of God. In a world of sin and hate it is difficult for us
to understand who the God of love is. These distortions interfere with our ability to express
our feelings to God and to trust him. This guide helps us to identify the distortions we have
and to come to a new understanding of who God is. Six studies, 64 pages, 1152-4.

Recovery from Distorted Images of Self. God created us as people who are to be loved, valued
and capable. But sometimes we don't *feel* that we are really cared for. We mentally replay
negative feedback again and again. These studies will show you how to escape those negatives
and be restored to a true vision of yourself as a person of immense worth. Six studies, 64 pages,
1162-1.

Recovery from Family Dysfunctions. Dysfunctional patterns of relating learned early in
life affect all of our relationships. We trust God and others less than we wish. This guide
offers healing from the pain of the past and acceptance into God's family. Six studies, 64
pages, 1151-6.

Recovery from Fear. Our fears revolve around certain basic issues—intimacy, risk, failure,
loneliness, inadequacy and danger. But God offers us support, empowerment and courage to
face fear in all areas of life. This guide will help us discover how God can enable us to face
our fears. Six studies, 64 pages, 1160-5.

Recovery from Guilt. Guilt is a distress signal that warns us that something is wrong. If
we do not pay attention, we will continue in destructive ways. This guide offers help in working

through the pain of what we have done to ourselves and others. Using steps four through nine of the Twelve Steps in conjunction with Scripture, these studies offer hope and help to get beyond guilt to forgiveness. Six studies, 64 pages, 1163-X.

Recovery: A Lifelong Journey. Recovery requires a commitment to keep growing and changing through prayer and discipline. In this guide you'll see how the last three steps of the Twelve Steps provide a model for your lifelong journey of recovery. By following the disciplines of self-awareness, confession, seeking God and asking for guidance, you will find continued healing and growth. Six studies, 64 pages, 1166-4.

Recovery from Loss. Disappointment, unmet expectations, physical or emotional illness and death are all examples of losses that occur in our lives. Working through grief does not help us to forget what we have lost, but it does help us grow in understanding, compassion and courage in the midst of loss. This guide will show you how to receive the comfort God offers. Six studies, 64 pages, 1157-5.

Recovery from Shame. Shame is a social experience. Whatever its source, shame causes people to see themselves as unlovable, unworthy and irreparable. This guide will help you to reform your self-understanding in the light of God's unconditional acceptance. Six studies, 64 pages, 1153-2.

Recovery from Spiritual Abuse. Because of negative teaching we have received, many of us have learned that we have to earn our way with God. We have come to experience the Christian life as a burden—and a source of deep shame. Through these studies, we will discover that we can be healed of spiritual abuse and find freedom and grace in Christ. Six studies, 64 pages, 1159-1.

Recovery from Workaholism. Hard work results in promotions, raises and the respect of colleagues. More important, it fills the need we have to be needed. But overwork also eats away at marriage and family relationships, while making friendships outside the office nearly nonexistent. It can create health problems as well as spiritual struggles. This guide is designed to help you break free of workaholism and accept the rest that God offers. Six studies, 64 pages, 1164-8.